Marriage

Connection

... making it work

Compiled by

Dr. Annette M. West

All Bible scriptures/quotations are taken from the King James Version. Copyright 2003 by Thomas Nelson Inc.

Printed in the United States of America

Copyright 2020 by Annette West

Library of Congress Control Number: 2020924728

ISBN: 978-1-7320260-4-9

by *JATNE* **Publishing**

Writing Coach: Anna J. Small Roseboro
Editor: Yolanda Whitehead
Book Cover Designer: Nikki S. West

Spiritual – Christian – Marriage – Daily Living – Bible Study – Teaching Source –Empowerment

FOREWORD

Nothing is more important than a love that lasts. It's not the most important thing, but it's up there! More than mere satisfaction (and that's a huge benefit), having the right person to share life with is critical. According to Dana Adam Shapiro's research for his book, You Can Be Right (or You Can Be Married), very few married people are happy — he says about 17 percent. This is an unbelievable finding! Yet in my work I have seen countless amount of people who are dissatisfied in their marriages and relationships.

When your marriage is a bad one it can have an effect on your emotions, health, finances, children and community at large. People who are married are less likely to have mental issues; that is if their marriage is a good one and enjoy psychological and emotional well-being. You are less likely to feel lonely. However, being unsatisfied in your marriage will eventually affect your mental health. One may develop anxiety, be depressed, make poor decisions and disrupt their sleeping patterns. Stress in one's marriage can develop harmful habits in their partner, increase heart disease, weaken the immune system, slow healing and increase diabetes. A bad marriage can affect your ability to build wealth, take advantage of insurance and tax benefits and even how your retirement planning turns out.

Children are the greatest casualty in bad marriages. Children can begin to "act out", become depressed and develop a myriad of behavioral problems. When there is constant fighting in the home children find ways to express their feelings and often the ways that are chosen can be detrimental.

According to recent research, 42-45% percent of first marriages end in divorce. 60% of second marriages end in divorce. 73% of third marriages end in divorce. Why is there so much heartache and lack of success in marriage? Marriage requires work, but unlike most beliefs, I don't think most of the work needs to be done during the marriage as much as it needs to be done BEFORE the marriage.

Do the work necessary BEFORE marriage to reduce the amount of work you will need to do later. In my work as a Christian premarital counselor and as the founder of the Wise Courtship Philosophy Group, I've noticed the need for individuals to do personal work on themselves first and proceed to learn skills in finding the right individual to share their life with. Far too often couples are more concerned with physical features, careers, status and emotional feelings when it comes to choosing a mate. These attributes can be a benefit but do not substitute a person's character and intentions.

I have spent a life encouraging those in the market of love and marriage to do the work up front BEFORE marriage. Do it for yourself, your future children, your health and finances. You are worth it!

The stories in this book share the ups and downs these couples had to endure to be successful in their marriage. Some are stories of heartbreak and triumph. Read them. Learn from them. Use the testimonies from these stories to help you to become all that GOD has called you to be. A great marriage will empower you to develop into your optimal self, productive and ever growing. Your marriage, done correctly and thoughtfully will be an example to the outside world of GOD's love on the earth. An example of love, forgiveness and unity.

Your choices will dictate the outcome of your life. Choose well and live!

Toni Henderson-Mayers
Relationship and Business Expert

DEDICATION

To couples striving daily to make a difference in their marriages, weathering the storms that arise and committed to staying connected to their spouse, and to those considering marriage get ready to embrace transformation in your relationships.

ACKNOWLEDGEMENTS

I acknowledge the love and support of my spouse, John. He is a blessing to my life and has put up with me for thirty-six years of marriage. Part of our marriage connection is seen in our working as a team when we attended a paint class where we created the birds for the cover of the book. Your love and support helps me daily to reach my aspirations. I love you!

To Anna J. Small Roseboro. We have a special-spiritual-sister connection. You are truly a Godsend to me and JATNE Publishing Company. I appreciate your willingness to share from the depth of wisdom and knowledge you possess.

To my daughters Nikki West and Yolanda Whitehead, and my sister Tuesday Payne. I can always call, text, email to get your input. You step in and help to get it done with successful outcomes. I appreciate and love you three dearly.

To the contributing authors. Without you this book would not have come to fruition. Thank you for sharing your story with the world. I pray God's riches blessings in your marriages.

Table of Contents

INTRODUCTION

Two come together, connecting, committing, making it work.

Come on, yes, you! Yeah, you did it! You said it, "I do." Now, what's next? Jump in and start reading the first chapter so you can see how the authors share their life with you. If you are willing to journey with us and hear our stories you will be enriched. You will see that it is possible to muddle through marriage and come out alright.

Being married, a person may think everything will be great once they say, "I do." However, the reality of marriage is it requires two people from different backgrounds coming together.

The first marriage ordained by God was in the Garden of Eden. Adam and Eve were the first man and woman and belonged to each other.

And the LORD God said, It is not good that the man should be alone; I will make him an help meet for him.
Genesis 2:18

The description in this passage of the original marriage is the basis for much of everything else the Bible says about marriage.

This is a practical resource tool for married couples, those considering marriage. Pastoral counselors and marriage coaches will find the content applicable to their clients.

If the reader is serious about having a *marriage connection*, this book will help towards that goal, moving to the next level in nurturing and building with their spouse. Investing energy to make a relationship that lasts a lifetime which requires time, energy, and resources for healthy outcomes.

How to Use This Book

This book has stories from the life and heart of the authors. Each couple presents content as they are led, which brings variety to the book flow. There is, also, a poetry section that will enrich your thoughts. The stories are ideal for leisurely reading, marriage and group discussion or Bible study. Prior to beginning the book, take the time to pray to the Lord to reveal what He would have you glean from this anthology.

- *Read* and *enjoy* each story.
- *Answer* the question(s) that follow.
- *Reflect* on the story. Summarize your thoughts and list the key points you recall.

- *Read* and *enjoy* the affirmation that follows each story.
- *Read* and *meditate* on the Scriptures for Further Study that follow each story.
- *Ponder* the poems in the poetry section. Reflect on ways they speak to you.
- *Draft* your own ACROSTIC poem about a person you would like to honor.
- *Read* the poem in the AFTERWORD.
- *Say* the Prayer in the AFTERWORD.
- *Learn* more about our contribution writers in the author section.

Blended. Now What?

Mochamad Usmanto and Mary Riley

To speak evil of no one, to be peaceable, gentle, showing all humility to all men.

Titus 3:2

Honestly, I didn't want to have anything to do with my ex-husband after we broke up. I was hurt, disappointed, and angry. For me, if the children never saw him, it was okay.

Here I am, sitting in my car, listening to music, waiting for my children. Not pleased with where I am at this point in my life. Having to pick my children up from their father's house, he shared with the woman he had an affair with before we divorced.

Such angry thoughts are shooting through my mind. Why did my now ex trade me in for a newer model, someone younger? I'm not too fond of the way she does my daughter's hair. The food she feeds them is not what I would give them.

There were other insignificant things that I held against her.

In my mind, there was nothing that I liked about her. This woman was younger than me. Her hair was wavy, and she wore it in two long braids. I thought she had lovely, natural hair. Up close to her, the aroma of her perfume reminded me of maple syrup, very sweet-smelling. The clothes she wore, the way she dressed showed her curves. She had my husband, and my children seemed to like her.

This alternative world he created, my new reality, included her, him, and four children now instead of only two. Because of how our marriage ended, and a bitter divorce, I let emotions, pain, hurt rule my thoughts and decisions in that season.

I didn't want to say that he was a good father or the other woman a wonderful mother.

My anger was clouding my best judgment. With all the negative thoughts running around in my head, saying anything good about them would not happen.

During this angry period after my divorce, I started spending time with the Indonesian community in my neighborhood, where they included me in their family. We would eat dinner as a family every Tuesday. The food they would cook was flavorful with rich flavors that varied from savory, hot and spicy, and sweet and sour.

One gentleman part of the community was the local sushi chef. He was young, handsome, and had a rock star look with a bit of hip-hop swag. His personality was upbeat, focused, and always joyful. This tall Indonesian man had light golden-brown skin with long straight black hair, twelve years younger than I, and a muscular body to wrap this incredible, attractive package up.

This young man had a love and reverence for God that I admired. He was kind, giving, and a loveable spirit, which caught my attention. I caught his eye. He asked me on a date, which was approximately a year after knowing each other. After that first date, we spent every day together.

Several months later, on August 11th of that year, which was my birthday, he looked at me with his intense, dark eyes and said, "I don't want you to date anyone else but me. I love you and want to spend the rest of my life treating you like a queen as you deserve. Would you marry me?" I was shocked and ecstatic at the same time because I loved him and didn't want to be with anyone else. I married this man with a beautiful spirit three months later in the northern Arkansas mountains during a small intimate destination wedding.

From the beginning of our relationship, he accepted my children as his own. He routinely calls them to check on their well-being, remembers their birthdays, and is always available to them in whatever capacity is needed. The relationship between my children and their new dad is so close. They often call him before they reach their biological father when they need advice, help, or someone to listen to them.

Initially, the relationship between my new husband and my children was not received well by my ex at all. My ex complained about everything dealing with my new husband, although they had never met. He disliked that our children were spending a lot of time with him. He resented that they felt more comfortable talking with their stepdad than him. My ex's insecurities created a lot of friction within our family.

My husband and I prayed together, sought guidance on how we should get along as one big cohesive family. We decided it was time for my ex to meet my husband.

When we gathered, my husband greeted my ex with an enormous hug. He said to him, "I love your children who are now my children, and you are a part of my children, which means I love you." Lord knows, conviction hit my inner being.

Lessons Learned

I treated my ex-husband's girlfriend the same way my ex was talking about my new husband. My behavior had set a nasty and negative tone. Thus, I chose not to speak negatively about my ex or his girlfriend after that moment.

Since love is unconditional and my new husband could show it to me and my ex, I needed to extend it to my ex and his girlfriend. I chose not to tear them down with negative words but be an advocate for them.

I chose to respect the ex and his girlfriend and not try to get into how they run their house. Realizing they are the ones that take care of my children when they are in that home. When I looked back and was honest with myself, the new girlfriend treated my children as if they were her own.

Now we all have a great relationship. We regularly get together as one enormous family. If it weren't for God, this would not have been possible. I thank God daily that we are examples of a happy blended family.

Also, I have chosen not to hold on to old stuff. It weighs heavily on the spirit. I was burdened down for a long time as I moaned, groaned, complained, and fed on negative thoughts. Now, I choose to look beyond the wrongs, stop finding fault, and respect my ex's new relationship.

Take caution with negative words, as children are always watching. Listening and may use that to their advantage. Even the slightest hint of vindictiveness can have long-term repercussions for children.

I acted out of anger. Hurt impeded my walk as a Christian and my role as a godly parent. I learned to stay focused and allow the Holy Spirit to guide me to do what is right.

Only through prayer and studying God's Word were we able to co-parent effectively. We all don't have to be friends; we don't even have to like each other. However, we owe it as Christian parents to walk in love and peace to provide a healthy environment for our children to thrive.

Below is a focus Scripture that helped us through this season.

God to give you a renewed
mind, heart, and spirit.
Romans 12:2

Blending families can be a beautiful experience. If a person is experiencing bitterness, jealously and resentment like I felt, seek the Lord in prayer. Read up on co-parenting books and magazines. Whatever it takes, the goal is to make it work. Harmony in the marriage is essential. However, if the conversation is always about the ex and their life, there will be significant issues to arise.

The Bible will help one deal with whatever is hindering them from walking in love. Through this blended family ordeal, I learned ways to refocus and believe they can help the reader on their journey. The following points should help you immensely.

Key Points for Blending Families

- Be kind to the ex-spouse.
- Be kind to the person the ex is dating.
- Choose not to be bitter.
- Say positive things about the other person to the children.
- Resentment tears down the spirit
- Love unconditionally

Respond Here

What behavior is keeping you from being the parent you want to be to your children or stepchildren?

_____

_____

_____

What is keeping you from getting along with your ex's spouse?

_____

_____

_____

How do you think God feels when you disrespect your ex?

_____

_____

_____

Share two positive ways you can have a better relationship with the ex and or their friend/spouse?

1. _____

_____

2. _____

_____

Now that you have read this story, write a brief statement on how you can create a well-blended family connection.

_____

_____

_____

_____

_____

_____

_____

_____

_____

_____

_____

_____

_____

Affirmation

I will treat others as I want them to treat me,
including the one the ex-spouse is with.

Scriptures for Further Study

Titus 3:2

To speak evil of no one, to be peaceable, gentle, showing all humility to all men

Romans 12:2

And be not conformed to this world: but be ye transformed by the renewing of your mind, that ye may prove what is that good, and acceptable, and perfect, will of God.

The Line in the Sand

Tommy and Michelle Russell

He that saith he abideth in Him ought himself
also to walk, even as He walked.

1 John 2:6

"He loves me; He loves me not" became the song of my heart every time I had a boyfriend. So, when Tommy and I met in the Fall of 1993, it did not differ from before. My best friend and roommate introduced us.

Here is where it all began for Tommy and me. My roommate's boyfriend and Tommy were friends and co-workers. They would ride together to work, and often they would stop by the smelly old apartment after work. As time passed, I finally got my first; "Can I take you on a date?" I was so excited; I didn't even ask where we were going. I just batted my dreamy eyes and said, sure! The club it was, and I wasn't even the club type. I thought, "He loves me, he loves me not," danced around in my forest of a mind! When we arrived at the club, others we knew enjoyed hardcore drinks as I sipped on a lovely frosty grape soda, gazing into Tommy's eyes. Then we glided to that old slippery club floor, intoxicating thoughts of being in love flood my mind!

There, I was a born-again Christian living a two-faced lifestyle, happily being pursued by this caramel-colored man! I did not ask him, "are you saved?" or better yet, do you believe in God? We never asked those questions.

He thought I was cute! I found him to be sharp, attractive; fine! After knowing each other for less than a year, we blindly move in together. We lived in an old two-story apartment building in a small town in South Carolina called Kingstree. We thought our life was good in that old smelly apartment. It was cold in the winter and steaming hot in the summer. Yes, we settled for a temporary image of a marriage. Things quickly down spiraled! We needed boundaries in our life. The revelation came, but our mind was short circuit by being caught up with life and our image.

Late one night, the phone rang. I raced to answer it and said, "hello!" A soft-spoken voice whispered, "Will you marry me," as it rippled through the telephone line. Tommy? Yes, it's me! Desperately, I replied, "will I marry you?" Then there was complete silence for a moment! Stop playing around, Tommy, and why aren't you here? I'm serious, Michelle, will you marry me? My voice slurred, yes!

Finally, he proposed, we were officially engaged! This proposal gave us a false sense of entitlement. As a result, we continued being sexually intimate, and I became pregnant. We were engaged but not yet married! We both agreed it was time to stop living together until marriage.

So, I went back home to live with my parents. Our daughter was born in June 1994. Then the emotions of being compelled to get married invade our minds. Despite all the red flags, we said, "I do!" and tied the knot on July 3rd, 1995.

We then created bills we could not manage! We had a wedding we could not afford. The courthouse would have made more sense. We had no bars, no barriers! There were no visible lines marked in the sand for us.

A line in the sand is a metaphor for creating limits. But when the boundaries established are crossed, it causes trouble.

The first line we drew in the sand was to stop living together until marriage, eliminating a false sense of entitlement to each other sexually outside of marriage.

The second line drawn in the sand was to stop making unwise spending decisions—a prescription for any marriage catastrophe.

Now we understand that healthy boundaries are partitions that establish expectations and show reverence for others. Biblical boundaries reflect self-regulation. Self-control is a product of the spirit.

After facing the debt that we accumulated because of lack of self-control playing the role of marriage back in that old smelly old apartment where we first met, it became clear. Healthy boundaries help create a line drawn in the sand against walking in the flesh's lust, the craving of the eye, the pride of life. We were using no counsel of God to guide our behavior or choices.

God gives free-will; we choose to live within His boundaries or outside of them. Tommy and I spent most of our free-will settling outside of them.

The reality of our decisions hit us! Freshly, married with no clue of what we had just done. Time unlocks the hidden vault of secrets that were accumulated over the years before we met. These secrets undermined our marriage in ways that you could not imagine!

Our house (lives) constructed on sand continued to sink! It needed the existence and authority of God! The best agreement we made personally and as a couple was inviting God back into our souls and our marriage. He is now the unseen spirit and change in our hearts that pushes us to set the barriers we need.

Lesson Learned

Tommy and I learned to measure our patterns to set godly boundaries, where we needed to draw the line on our behaviors. There is safety being inside God's limits that produce grace, but living outside of them brings disorder and bewilderment.

As we developed in our conviction in God, we learned that making God first is our preference. We both required the technique of setting boundaries in our lives. Therefore, we felt the need to look to God and lean not to our intelligence.

For instance, after having our daughter, we realized that God had blessed us with a beautiful baby. We quickly realized that to raise her and protect her; we could not continue to walk outside the counsel of God.

We sought God! To identify which barriers to set, we had to study how to interact and be straightforward about telling the truth in love, even when it stings! The Bible encourages us to tell the truth in love. Hearing the truth from each other that sometimes we both feel unappreciated by the other is invariably unpleasant! But it was for our maturity and not for scorn. We didn't need to exhaust time setting boundaries on a fraudulent instruction. But on principles established in God's message that can provide stable results. This refining is never easy. But we now seek it! We have set precise and healthy boundaries that reveal what is and what is not admissible.

For instance, we refuse to ignore the others' feelings, even if we disagree. But we agree to listen.

God moved us to go on a 40-day challenge to fireproof our marriage! It was a fiction book recommended to us by pastor friends of ours. But it remained on the bookshelf, collecting duct. It stayed there for about seven years. But after a nasty argument concerning an old unrelated issue, we blasted the grime off the book and got to work.

We are keeping God first, setting the right boundaries! Here is a focal Scripture we have used in guiding our growth and learning to put things in proper perspective.

But the fruit of the spirit is love, joy, peace, forbearance, kindness, goodness, faithfulness, gentleness and self-control. Against such things there is no law.

Galatians 5:22-23

It's safe to say that our marriage is fireproof! Today, "He loves me, He loves me still" is the song of our heart. Dedicate to the Lord!

Key Points to Setting Boundaries

- Be wise and don't spend beyond your income.
- Self-control helps keep finances in order.
- Failure is not a choice. Whatever it takes, that is godly; put in the work.
- Work together as a team for success.

Respond Here

Define boundary from a Biblical viewpoint.

_____

_____

_____

_____

_____

_____

When a conversation turns out of control with your mate, what should the next step be?

_____

_____

_____

_____

_____

Read Proverbs 16:32. Write two barriers you can set after reviewing this Scripture.

1.

_____

_____

2.

_____

_____

Now that you have read this story, write a brief statement on how you can establish better boundaries in your habits.

_____

_____

_____

_____

_____

_____

_____

_____

_____

_____

_____

_____

Affirmation

I will make wise choices in spending so that resources are not wasted.

Scriptures for Further Study

Proverbs 21:5

The thoughts of the diligent tend only to plenteousness; but of every one that is hasty only to want.

1 Corinthian 1:10

Now I beseech you brethren, by the name of our Lord Jesus Christ, that ye all speak the same thing, and that there be no divisions among you, but that ye be perfectly joined together in the same mind and same judgement.

Things Are Different Now

Charles and Lekeisha Mosley

Train up a child in the way he should go: and when he is old, he will not depart from it.

Proverbs 22:6

Growing up in the cold, wintertime was fun and exciting in the brisk Motown City of Detroit, Michigan. In the fluttering snow, what fun, spinning around, lying down on the lawn to make snow angels, and throwing snowballs at the kids in the neighborhood. Life was good.

I knew that even though he had worked hard all day when he came home, my father would get the snow shovel out of the garage and clear the way. He would joyfully shove the snow from the sidewalks in front of our home. In the Eastside neighborhood where we lived, the city snowplows came through, pushing the snow on the street, often trapping cars along the curb. My dad made sure our pathways were clear to the car and out in front of our house. Shoveling snow is just one way my father made sure we were safe in and around our home. Because he strove to do what he could to ensure clear paths along the way, I have become the woman I am today.

I married Dwayne and bore him two sons. But, the marriage did not last. Eventually, however, the Lord blessed me to meet and marry Charles, a man I soon realized had traits similar to my father. Charles had grown up and been raised in Michigan by his mother, Francine. Her husband had left her to take care of four girls and one boy.

His mother worked with very little money, and the family survived and thrived. This family of six-feet tall members stuck together like glue! For years, Charles was the only male child in the family, until his mother remarried and had another boy, but then Charles had left for college.

Mutual friends set us up for a blind date. "Charles is a great guy!" they said. "And, he has no children." I took a chance and went out with him. We hit it off great and kept regular contact with each other. By then, he lived in Maryland, and I was still in Michigan. Two years later, we said, "I do."

We both are private people inclined to keep our marital business within our home. Once, we became a blended family with the sons from my previous marriage and their father, Dwayne, who wished to remain involved in their lives. My boys now have a second father. We are blessed because my husband became the bonus dad, excited to be an addition to our lives. But our family soon faced issues of joint child-rearing to consider.

Charles did not grow up with his father in the house. Though my husband did not have a role model, he was willing to seek mentors from the males in our church; he was open to their guidance as he assumed this double new role of husband and father.

Changing thought processes and behaviors are critical to making it work in our marriage. My husband had to adjust to being a father; I had to adapt to a new husband's opinions. This period in our lives became a slippery time of trial and error. Family decisions required new understanding from each of us as issues arose related to disciplining our sons.

We both acknowledged, "Things are different now." To have a successful marriage, we have learned to work as a team and remain flexible. Issues arose when we made choices based on our experiences growing up in very different households. We needed to agree as a couple and sometimes as a triple. We also saw that Dwayne, Sr. the boys' dad, needed to be involved at times.

I thought I knew best about marriage and child-rearing. After all, I was tempted to exclaim, "I have been married before. I am their mother!". But I also am married to a new man. I respect him. That means I must listen and sometimes consent to his ways of handling situations.

Some disagreements arise over petty issues, like slick, icy spots on a city sidewalk of life, which can trip up a marriage. For instance, my husband, who works in the corporate world, believes appearance matters. So, for him, males wearing earrings is a "No, No!"

My oldest son Dewayne is a senior in high school. He is a high-energy teen who loves track and singing and wants to have fun without the restraint of parental boundaries. In our home, my husband said Dewayne was to remove his earrings when inside our home.

Before this incident, Charles and I had not discussed who and how we would discipline our children when they flouted house rules. This incident evoked action. Charles and I conversed awhile and worked it out. We agreed. "If our son gets his ears pierced, he had better not come in this house wearing earrings!".

Dewayne, Jr. protested. He kept on his earrings. When confronted, he rebounded, "I'm going to ask my father!" I spoke with my son's father. Thankfully, Dwayne, Sr. honored Charles and me and supported our decision. He talked to his namesake and advised him to abide by the "house rules." Of course, Dewayne Jr. was not happy, but he conceded. He recognized the power of a united team of parents.

Wow, a slippery moment avoided! My sons now have two dads. We parents are learning to work in harmony and see that the adults talking to each other can clear the way and solve issues quicker.

I sometimes reflect on the new challenges that arose in our blended marriage. Many parenting decisions confront us, inherent with raising growing boys through phases in friendships, enemies, relationships, and physical fitness. I am tempted to step in and intervene like a momma bear. Of course, "I'm their mother! I know best!" or so I thought. However, more and more often, I have allowed my husband to lead.

Over time, Charles and I established house rules. One rule is that the boys are expected to check with us before leaving the house and can go only after completing their homework and chores. Our oldest son chose not to follow the rules.

When my husband called him on it, our son responded defiantly. At times like this, Dewayne usually wanted to bring in his biological father to stand in his corner. This tendency proved problematic—another icy patch. My husband's goal is to have peace in the family. More often now, we explain to our sons the rationale for the rules we establish for them. We strive to do it the Bible way.

Train up a child in the way he should go
and when he is old, he will not depart from it.
Proverbs 22:6

I love that my husband is good at not comparing our marriage and raising our boys the way others' do. He and I work toward flexibility in decision making, often with compromises or concessions. I trust my husband's authority as our household leader. I know him to be an honorable man and have faith in him to make decisions that will benefit our marriage connection.

Like my father, Charles has a quiet way of doing what must be done to clear the way. When life seems like a snowstorm creating slippery walkways, where we could stumble, fall, and fail as a family, my husband readily steps up to do what is necessary for our safety and security. Charles, a man, raised in a home without a father, cheerfully listens and learns, dependably advises based on Biblical principles, and stands firm in his faith. I, too, have learned that God has connected me with a man who had no children of his own, yet married me, a divorced mother of two sons. He loves my children and respects my experience as their mother. Things genuinely are different now

Key Thoughts for Decision-making

- Know that change is inevitable and can be a good thing.
- Be willing to listen to the spouse for direction.
- Realize it's a learning process, and you don't have all the answers.
- Don't bring a plan from a prior marriage.
- Seek God for direction and clarity in decision-making.

Respond Here

How can you honor your spouse in their way of disciplining children?

_____

_____

_____

_____

If a conversation spins out of control with your children, what solution do you seek?

_____

_____

_____

_____

When a situation arose that was concerning our son Dewayne, his father would get involved. Do you believe the opinion of the ex-husband matters?

_____

_____

_____

_____

Now that you have read this story, write a brief statement on how you can communicate better in your decision-making.

_____

_____

_____

_____

_____

_____

_____

_____

_____

_____

_____

_____

_____

Affirmation

I will trust my spouse in how decisions are made to develop our children that honor God.

Scriptures for Further Study

Ephesians 6:1-3

Children should be obedient to and honor their parents, as long as the parents do not ask the children to do anything against God's will

Titus 2:3-5

A woman should teach others what is good, carry herself modestly and submissively, and train younger women how to love their husbands and children.

Fool, Be Gone

John and Annette West

Be ye angry, and sin not.

Ephesians 4:26a

In the summer of 1982, I met John in my neighborhood, Pine Chapel, the projects to be exact. He sought me out, and we talked—a military man with a friendly personality. As we spent time together, my thoughts were not on a long-term relationship or marriage.

I liked my life as a single mother of two children. I was holding down my household. Again, let me say he was soft-spoken, pleasant and the conversation stimulating. We began talking about life and our goals, and gradually, my thoughts shifted to "maybe he's a keeper."

Through conversations, we realized we had much in common. We wanted a home and not just a house. A place without hollering and screaming.

Respect and not speaking harshly to each other. Also, we had similar thoughts on ways of child-rearing. We knew for sure that the love of God would be the answer to help us through our journey.

Guess it was destiny, God-ordained, because it came to be. We chose a Wednesday evening to marry so that our close-knit church family could attend just before bible study.

We had a simple wedding as money was minimal. Willie, my baby sister, was maid of honor, and John's friend, Jim, best man. My Grammie, Auntie Linda, and Godfather, Mr. Flanagan, in his sharp suit and hat in attendance. Also, my year-apart twin, Tuesday, was there. That is a family joke because she was born on my first birthday, my gift.

Since money was sparse, our church gave us a small reception on Saturday, and my

Grammie and Auntie came. My mom was out of town on one of her conventions.

Now married, our family, John, me, and the two children, Terrance, seven, and Nikki, three, moved to Iceland. It was a beautiful place and very family-oriented. We connected with the same church denomination we attended in the states.

The complex we lived in was called Tree Housing. The apartments were spacious; children had separate bedrooms. Oh yes, they called it Tree Housing because each building was named after a tree. We lived in Elm Housing.

We could look down through the large windows in our home and see black shiny lava rock instead of grass. Standing there looking straight across the horizon, drew the eyes to brown jagged mountainous peaks with beautiful white pristine snow. It was so beautiful and peaceful.

The one thing I didn't like was those long winters. One day we were having only 30 minutes of sunlight. Dark when you go to bed, get up, go to work, leave work, and make it home. It definitely could lead to depression if one were not careful.

In this season of our marriage, we had a vibrant church life, prayed together, and lived a harmonious time connecting. My husband was active in ministry efforts. He attended men's study. He led Bible study in the home and prayed with and over the family. He even spoke, giving the Sunday message during service. My goodness, was I proud of him!

I taught Sunday School to the little ones and assisted in the adult study during the week.

We worked together; our priority was nurturing our two children. It was a beautiful life.

However, when things are going great, there can be a moment or season of disconnect. John and I talked before we got married to our expectations, yet we missed some things. Not fully understanding how our communication would determine if we were on a healthy part of our marriage.

Foolish Behavior and Words

Once we returned to the USA from Iceland and settled in our home, my husband's grandmother, Mawmaw, affectionately called, and a few cousins visited North Carolina. We had an enjoyable week together, and they would leave in another day.

My grandmother, Grammie, lived down the road, only a minute from me. Sunday afternoon was her group time. If my aunt were unavailable, I would take her.

When I returned from church service, I spoke with my husband to let him know my plans. Then I cooked dinner and washed clothes so his family would not take dirty clothes back with them. We are laughing and talking, enjoying the last day together.

It was about an hour before I was to take my Grammie to her group that John wanted to talk with me. He said both of us should drive to the bus station to see his family off. I said no.

In mind, my thought was, "I don't need to be at the train station to see them off. I don't want to drive 30 minutes away and through a tunnel. I don't like that tunnel, people driving at 55 miles an hour in a tube. Two tight lanes, no margin for error, wall on each side, and it's the only way to get to the train station." Yuk!

The time comes for me to pick up my Grammie. I walk to the kitchen, my hand reaching for the key. No key to be found. I ask John if he knows where my keys are.

He says something to the effect of "I don't like your attitude."

I'm thinking, what attitude, my opinion counts?

He says, "I asked you to go tomorrow, and you said no."

I'm thinking about what this got to do with my keys. I say again, "John, where are my keys." I'm guessing he's playing and put my keys in the car. My goodness, I was getting angry, stars in my eyes, a headache trying to come on as fire boils within me. The fool in me is getting ready to show up and act out. I go outside to the car.

John walks outside and sits in the passenger front seat.

I walk out the kitchen door, go around to the driver's side of the car, open the door, and take a seat. I'm checking to see if he put my keys in the car. Nope, no keys. I ask again for my keys. No response.

I look at him; he's calm, but I'm fuming. In my mind, I said, I'm not having anyone take anything from me. I don't want to give. I saw childhood drama and family abuse flash before my eyes. In this situation, I fought with words. I acted like a total fool. Every explicative that I didn't know was in me spewed out. I'm sure his family in the house heard me too.

My husband said not a word, his head hanging down, got out of the car, and walked into the house.

I got out of the car and sat in the carport. It took me some time to come down from that moment. What's funny is I didn't realize that I could act like that. We had never argued, never fussed in these two years dating, and two years married. Yes, we had some issues, but we had already said that we would not treat each other like children. However, at that moment, that is how I felt he treated me when he removed my keys and wouldn't give them back.

I was also frustrated because not having my keys kept me from picking my Grammie up, making her miss the group. I had made a promise to her, and she was waiting for me. It was significant for her, so it was essential for me too.

I sat in the car and fumed a bit, called my dad to come to pick me up, and was ready to pack my bags to leave. As I came down off my angry high, my foolish behavior, I realized that I had spoken out of my heart that which I didn't know was within. I displeased the Lord with my tone and words and hurt Johns' feeling. Yes, I would have to ask forgiveness from God and my spouse for my words spoken. It was okay to get angry, but not to act out on it. Paul addresses this in the following Scripture.

Be ye angry, and sin not: let not the sun
go down upon your wrath.
Ephesians 4:26

Now I'm not saying my spouse was right. He had no business taking anything of mine. However, what I'm saying is I still must look to my response, foolish behavior in that situation. How I behaved was out of my usual character, but I sinned and needed to repent.

Lesson Learned

As I recognized my shortcoming and went before the Lord, I asked the Lord to help me honor Him in all that I say and do, and then my spouse, as I would expect for myself. I cried within; I prayed to pull my mind back into focus.

A few hours later, I was ready to talk about my foolish behavior.

John said he took my keys because I wouldn't do what he wanted. He asked me to forgive him for his behavior and said he wouldn't do that again.

We forgave each other, and we have not acted that way since then. We shared our thoughts, cried, asked forgiveness, and prayed. I've never been one to hold a grudge, stay angry at anyone, so it was easy for me to move on. We did not let the sun go down with harsh feelings for one another.

From this foolish behavior moment, I realized the importance of saying what is on my mind to help the situation. Although I needed to say *no* about making the drive through the tunnel, I did not share the thoughts running around in my mind. In retrospect, what could have helped was me saying, I get nervous, am uncomfortable driving through the tunnel because I'm claustrophobic.

The following is a favorite Scripture that helped us through these thirty-six years of marriage, especially me.

Let no corrupt communication proceed
out of your mouth, but that which is good
to the use of edifying, that it may minister

grace unto the hearers.

Ephesians 4:29

As I took the time to seek the Lord after my unacceptable behavior, I sought to avoid going down that road again.

John and I learned that when a marriage begins, one or both parties may not know much. Initially, we didn't have anyone giving us direction to make a marriage connection. We were not in agreement with outside counseling. To help us, I did two things.

The first was reaching out to one a woman in the counseling department of our church. Having someone, I could ask questions. The second was purchasing books for us to read on marriage.

In that season of our marriage, we studied the bible, prayed together, and talked about what we were reading, which helped our marriage grow. The following list is key behaviors learned for healthier communication.

Key Points to Not Act Like a Fool

- Do not act out of emotions.
- Consider the words before speaking.
- Be angry, but don't act like a fool.
- Be willing to seek outside counseling or coaching.
- Invest in study materials to help strengthen your marriage.
- Spend time together and seek the Lord in all things.

Respond Here

Define communication.

_____

_____

_____

When conflict arises, how do you communicate with your spouse?

_____

_____

_____

Read Proverbs 12:8. Write positive words from this Scripture to use when you are angry?

_____

_____

_____

Read Ephesians 4:29. How can you connect better with your spouse from this verse?

_____

_____

_____

_____

What are two ways you can communicate better with your spouse?

1. _____

_____

2. _____

_____

Now that you have read this story, write a brief statement on how you can create healthier communication in your marriage.

_____

_____

_____

_____

_____

_____

_____

_____

_____

_____

_____

_____

_____

Affirmation

I will strive for effective communication to build a strong, healthy marriage.

Scriptures for Further Study

Proverbs 12:18

There is one whose rash words are like sword thrusts, but the tongue of the wise brings healing.

James 1:19

Know this, my beloved brothers: let every person be quick to hear, slow to speak, slow to get angry.

Together We Win

David and Tanika Blanding

How can two walk together except
they be agreed?
Amos 3:3

When I was a child, I always dreamed of one day getting married to my prince-charming, becoming the dearest mother of all. I grew up in a small town in the backwoods of what we called "potato creek." We had two stop signs and one caution light at the "crossroads." Down back in the woods behind the chicken coop and through the garden of collard greens, okras, and squash, lived my mom, dad, two siblings, and I. I was in the middle. We called it being the "Yellen baby." We lived in a long single-wide trailer, just a few muddy ditches behind my grandparent's house.

My siblings and some cousins, and I would find ourselves at Grandma's house more than we were at our own home. Grandma always seemed to be a very independent woman, delightfully carrying the weight of the world upon her shoulders. She still got things done in her strength. At grandma's house, I would learn the most critical values that would mold me into who I am today.

After graduating from high school, I went off to college and simultaneously joined the United States Army. I continued to develop an extraordinary friendship with a handsome young fellow named David that I had known in passing over the past 12 years. We knew each other through a mutual friend of a friend. I always thought he was cute. I dared to let him know. I didn't want him to think I liked him. Throughout my first semester in college, and even though basic combat training, I kept my calm and continued to be that friend he admired.

About a year later, David moved to New York. I missed him so much. We talked for hours on the phone about nothing. I could feel him breathing through the phone; the subtle sound of his lips pressed closely into the phone was so satisfying that I didn't mind wasting all of my minutes on my ten-dollar prepaid calling card.

In the summer of 2001, David came to visit me at my mother's house. I opened the door right away; he asked me if I wanted to take this friendship to the next level. My pride reared its non-emotional head; I said, "No, let's just be friends." To this day, I regret those words.

In time, the title "Friend" got old, so we made it official. On October 9th, 2004, we married. David vowed that he forgave me preemptively for anything that I may do in the future. I could not bring myself to vow the same thing. I wasn't even sure if I was going to be in this marriage forever. There I was, a young woman in her early 20s, with no clue what he meant about forgiving me always. In hindsight, I know what he was saying.

David would often repeat the phrase, "it's me and you against the world." I guess he was trying to prepare me for the opposition and remind me that we were stronger together. Those words meant nothing to me. I thought we would marry and live happily ever after. Boy, was I wrong. After only a few short months of being married, we got into a very heated argument about a job offer that I accepted. The position was for a convenient store clerk. Although this job had long hours with low pay, I felt that I just needed something to help pay the bills. Anything that brought legit money into the home was good enough for me.

As I get my words together to tell David my good news, I walk into the apartment and say, "David, I got the job; I start next week." I could see the look on his face of what appeared to be a disappointment. He immediately asked, "Why are you settling for this job, Nika?" I took offense to his comment. I started having vivid flashbacks of the independence of my grandmother. I felt I had to prove that I didn't need to depend on anyone to take care of me or help me decide. As my husband, David, should have been excited about me getting a job offer. After all, I was trying to be his helpmeet.

About 10 minutes after the argument, I stormed out of the apartment, went to my car, and called my mother. I told her every single detail of the fight. I told her everything that I felt in that moment, pouring out the pieces I felt would help my one-sided story.

Towards the end of the conversation, I felt pretty good to get things off my chest. I had someone willing to listen to me. Well, little did I expect, when I stopped yapping while taking a breath of fresh air, I silently heard those words that David had so faithfully spoken to me, "it's me, you against the world." In my mind, I thought, well, I just took all of my marital business and shared it with my mom. Now, I don't know what damage I may have caused in her heart towards her son-in-law. I felt like I had given her the ammunition, loaded the weapon, took it off the safety, and pulled the trigger for her feelings to unleash into that protective mommy mode. I would get over this argument within the next five minutes; my mom could potentially hold on to this for five years. Whew, I thank God this was not the case.

Riding the Bench

I compare this stage of my marriage to the game of basketball. As I sit and think about David's famous phrase, "it's me and you against the world." I see it as a metaphor that he used to express how close we should stick together regardless of the circumstances. In basketball, the team player has many choices, a willingness or refusal to accept the head coach's position offer. Our head coach is God, the Father. In the game of basketball, each position is played by a specific team member at a set time. If the player is not in the game, the coach will often ask the person to sit down or "ride the bench." I found myself at this point in our marriage in the wrong position. Riding the bench was very unfamiliar and uncomfortable for me.

Growing up as a child, I always saw my grandma on the court, dribbling, shooting, scoring points; she did it for the entire team. Her example of always getting it done by herself made me believe that I am a team of one.

In 2011, the Army reassigned me, David, and our two girls from Virginia to Maryland. After four years of being stationed at Fort Meade, Maryland, it was time to move to a new duty station. I hoped to move back to South Carolina to be closer to the family; I also felt God wanted to send us back home for a reason.

Towards the end of my tour, I reached out to the Human Resources Command, "HRC" to inquire about positions on Fort Jackson, SC. They informed me there were no positions for my rank. Instead, they offered me a job in Fort. Gordon, Georgia.

Although it wasn't what I wanted, I was pretty excited about the offer. I hung up the phone from the HRC personnel and immediately called David. As the phone is ringing and I anticipate him saying hello, I am rehearsing how lovely it will be to move to Georgia to get stationed closer to home. By the way, it was much better than getting moved out west, to what we call "in the middle, of nowhere." Once David picked up the phone, I expressed to him what HRC had brought to my attention. David's response was, "the next time we move, it's going to be us moving to South Carolina." Boy, was this a hard pill to swallow. I had gotten my hopes up to move to Georgia, the closest to South Carolina that we could get. He immediately shuts it down.

By now, I became offended. I said to David, "How could you say this when my career manager is telling me that there are no positions available in South Carolina?" Now I am stuck in a pickle. If I don't take Georgia, then I will have to take whatever else is available. I am back to feeling like how I felt in 2004 when we were arguing about me taking the job at the convenience store. I felt like he was trying to make decisions for me again. I am not having this. At this point, I am overwhelmed. I quickly hang up with David, close my office door, and began to cry. My heart was pounding like a bass drum in an apostolic church on a Friday night revival. I was stuck between what my husband heard God saying to him and what my career manager said; it's impossible. I remember wishing and hoping that David was 100% sure of what the Lord had been showing him because it was the complete opposite of what "man" said.

I began to feel weak over this life-changing decision. I slumped over in my black swiveled office chair and prayed as I had never prayed before. With my head lying over my dripping wet and snotty keyboard, my eyeballs burn from squeezing them closed so tight. I whispered, as my voice cracked from my vocal cords being strained. "Lord, I am. I am so scared right now. I am your daughter, and you said if I delight myself in you, you will give me the desires of my heart. Lord, please help me to trust that my husband is making the right decision for our family. Help me to be confident in the man that I am blessed to be married to. Lord, I need your help with setting my pride aside. Help me to hold out until you make this right for us." I prayed this prayer for weeks. I truly believed that God was going to work in our favor.

Now, riding the bench on this team became real. I had to wait and be patient. I called HRC back and told them that I would not be accepting Georgia as our next assignment. I was so afraid even after I prayed a prayer of faith. At this point, we have two kids and one on the way—no family within an eight-hour drive, with no telling where our next move will be. I had to wait it out and see how this game was going to play out—being so careful not to feel that David and I were opponents. I had to remind myself that we are on the same team and win this together. At this point, I was still riding the bench, but my position called for me to cheer my team to victory in the role of prayer.

A few months later, Memorial Day weekend, 2015, we visited our family in South Carolina. David went to a prayer meeting. He heard the Lord speak to him again, clearly concerning our move to South Carolina. I was, however, getting very anxious on the bench. I was hinting at the coach, God the Father, to put me in the game, feeling I could get the job done better than my teammate. Yet, the coach, God, said, "No, hold tight, I know what I'm doing. Continue to cover your position in prayer; be anxious for nothing." On the trip back to Maryland, our team rejoiced to know that we would soon have victory.

As we pulled into our driveway, I received a phone call from my career manager, offering me a position in Fort Jackson, SC. The first question from him, "How soon can you be in South Carolina?" My mouth dropped to what felt like the top of the kitchen floor. I couldn't believe my ears. He asked me to accept the position via phone tentatively, and he would send me the official offer to my email. I stalked my email for what seemed like the next 12 hours. By October 2015, we had our entire house packed along with two kids, a 7-month-old belly, driving down Interstate 95 South.

Make the Dream Work

I believe our coach, God the Father, was convinced I had learned the importance of my position while riding the bench, cheering my teammate forward. Once I was ready to get back on the court, God led us on a unique assignment. The reward gained for our obedience in moving as a team. We founded a non-profit corporation called Creating Miracles Life-Changing Corporation. The organization was officially established in April 2016 to restore communities to a place of self-sufficiency. By September 3rd, 2016; we had our first annual back to school event. It turned out to be one of the most significant events held in the Summerton community. We had over 500 personnel in attendance, support from all facets of life. During this event, people registered to vote; high schoolers signed for college, some signed to join the Armed Forces, some volunteered at the local Fire Department. It was in this year that God showed me what it meant to be a real "team player." Now that we both understood the effectiveness of us moving as a team made room for us to grow in other areas. As needed, we would be prepared to switch to different positions required to keep our team winning.

In the year 2017, we started a weekly podcast called "Till Death Do Us Part," which reaches thousands of people across the country. We are at liberty to share our life experiences with the world, to encourage people to live their best life beyond the odds they may face. Through this God-ordained platform, people are healed, delivered, made free.

In this year of 2017, I learned that every position on our team is essential. Being attentive to my teammate, recognizing the areas he needs strength in is crucial. Like in the basketball game, it doesn't matter if you are a center, forward, pointing guard, shooting guard, or even riding the bench; the most critical piece in teamwork is taking instructions from the coach. This is important, so one teammate won't be playing the wrong position at the wrong time. That can cause the entire team to lose the game. Scripture tells us why two are better than one.

Two are better than one; because they have a
good reward for their labor. For if they fall, the
one will lift up his fellow: but woe to him that is
alone when he falleth; for he hath not another to
help him up. Again, if two lie together, then they
have heat: but how can one be warm alone? And
if one prevail against him, two shall withstand
him; and a threefold cord is not quickly broken.

Ecclesiastes 4:9-12

Tanika's Reflection

Growing up with such a powerful woman in my life, like my grandmother, largely influenced me always to feel the need to do everything on my own. I developed a fear of sharing responsibility. To me, if I weren't in control, things would not be done correctly. I had a tough time trusting my husband's word over my own. With an independent mindset for so many years, I wasn't fair to my teammate. And I was overexerting myself. By the grace of God, I have learned that it's okay to ride the bench sometimes.

Sometimes in the marriage, both parties have to step back, take some time, and rethink past behaviors. We need a brief break to catch our breath, gather our thoughts. Just as in the game of basketball, the ability to ride the bench, trusting teammates can take you through the rest of the time on the clock is part of playing.

I didn't understand that teamwork sometimes required compromise, and for my team to win the game against the adversary, we had to play together. In my case, the adversary was pride and fear, trusting that God would carry me through the most humbling and unassuming times in my life. In this experience, I realized that I didn't have to control the ball to be actively playing the game, as long as my teammate and I stuck together, no matter what the world said, thought, or did. We must keep receiving our instructions from the head coach, focus on the end state, and always work together. This game plan, which develops in the locker room of prayer, will always guarantee victory on the full court.

Key Thoughts for Teamwork in Marriage

- Keep your team's developing plan in the locker room (relationship)
- Take instructions from the Coach and Assistant Coach (God, Husband)
- Do not be afraid to not be in control
- Ride the Bench (Stay in prayer.)
- Remember that you and your teammate are on a mission to tackle the opponent together. One Team, One Fight.

Respond Here

What is teamwork in a marriage? Share an example of teamwork in your marriage.

_____

_____

_____

How important are the positions on the team in your marriage?

_____

_____

_____

What are some distractions that may cause your team to lose focus on the game (marriage goal)?

_____

_____

Recall a time where you were not an outstanding player on the team?

_____

_____

_____

What are two ways that you can become a better team player?

1. _____

_____

2. _____

_____

Now that you have read the story, write a brief statement about how you can be an effective team player?

_____

_____

_____

_____

_____

_____

_____

_____

_____

_____

_____

_____

Affirmation

*I will daily work on my marriage
to build up our team.*

Scriptures for Further Study

Ecclesiastes 4:9-10

Two are better than one; because they have a good reward for their labour. For if they fall, the one will lift up his fellow: but woe to him that is alone when he falleth; for he hath not another to help him up. (Read versus 11-12)

Psalms 133:1

Behold, how good and how pleasant it is for brethren to dwell together in unity!

Sex Me More!

Terrance and Yolanda Whitehead

Defraud ye not one the other, except it, be with consent for a time, that ye may give yourselves to fasting and prayer; and come together again, that Satan tempt you not for your incontinency.

1 Corinthians 7:5

Have you ever listened to a married couple tell a story? You will often get a little of the story from her perspective and a little from his. If told in one sitting, you may even enjoy the back and forth between the two. We choose to tell our story in this manner.

Her Story

My husband and I are what people refer to as "High School Sweethearts." As teenagers, we thought we knew it all and planned our life together. Mostly, we stuck to that plan. He enlisted in the Air Force right after graduation. Later, I followed him to his first base, where I enrolled in a local college. After a few bumps in the road, we married at the young age of 21. We waited until I finished college to start a family and checked all the boxes - had two children, bought a house, two cars, and a dog. From the outside looking in, we were the perfect little family. However, problems arose in our marriage. Instead of talking about them and working together to overcome our struggles, we looked the other way. After 15 years of marriage, we separated and began the process of divorce. But God.

His Story

When I first saw my wife, I was 16 years young, full of hormones, and full of ambition. Shortly after we met, she became my girlfriend and then my best friend. From our senior year in high school to now, we have grown together, apart, and together again. We've honestly done that more than a few times, but here we are.

The journey has been short of perfection, lacking understanding and honesty, BUT GOD. Our story is like the old rhyme, sugar, and spice, and everything nice. Our smorgasbord of a relationship has just the right amount of history, hurt, and healing that has propelled us toward genuine love and sharing.

Her Story

After three and a half years of separation, we made a new commitment to one another as God restored our relationship. I often refer to our marriage as the before and after, the first half and the second half. We have experienced a shift in our relationship.

The most significant change is that we have allowed God to be the center of our lives individually and the center of our marriage. The second most crucial shift is communication. For this second half of our marriage to be the best possible, we have had to confront those problems we initially tried to sweep under the rug. We had to acknowledge the elephants in the room and work together to get rid of them for good. Some of these conversations were difficult. One of the most difficult conversations of all has been about sex.

His Story

As a young man in my teens and then into my early twenties and even thirties, I thought sex was a given for two people in a relationship. I don't know if I ever truly understood the intimacy that goes into making sure my spouse was comfortable and felt wanted by me.

I failed on many levels, but I didn't truly comprehend where the two of us had failed one another until recently. I never knew that having an intimate relationship with my God would allow me to right my wrongs, identify my false truths, and connect with my wife. As I built upon my relationship with Him, I noticed that my wife's understanding and appreciation became more evident, and her purpose and ours were more substantial. I hoped for an opportunity to rectify a broken home and lived in the moment, allowing God to work in our situation.

Her Story

Yes, let's talk about sex, shall we? As with most married couples with children, we are

TIRED. It's challenging to find time for intimacy. We both have acknowledged that one issue in the first half of our marriage was that we put our intimacy and connection on the back burner.

This time around, we know we must do all we can to put our relationship first (after God, of course). God designed sex to be the ultimate connection between a husband and wife. There are several forms of intimacy, but sex is the one thing that we felt we needed most. As we began talking about the importance of a healthy sexual relationship, an ugly elephant arose and demanded our attention.

His Story

The issue with sex is that it is societally categorized as the norm, something given in any relationship between a man and a woman, married or not. The world bombards us with music lyrics, movies, television, and images in the media centered on sex. For men, these speak to the fantasy of sex. For women, these speak to the romance of sex. My wife and I never discussed sex in terms of what God intended it to be because we didn't have a firm grasp on this ourselves.

Her Story

As a young teenage girl, I was looking for love in all the wrong places. I didn't know my value and did not have a relationship with the Lord. I fell into some unhealthy relationships as I continued to look to others for validation. One of these relationships would include a sexual experience that has never left me.

Recently, I heard the term "grey area of consent." This "grey area" is when an individual doesn't necessarily say no to a sexual encounter. Still, he/she doesn't say yes either. At a young age, I experienced a situation that I now understand was a "grey area of consent." Afterward, I would walk away bruised, both physically and mentally, and feeling ashamed. It has come to light that this one shameful sexual experience has been with me for over 25 years and has impacted my sexual relationship with my husband.

His Story

It takes a mature man and woman in a relationship to open up, lay it all on the table, and give it to God. My wife and I attempted to open up during the first half of our marriage. Still, we fell short by holding back the essential experiences. Maybe we were scared, ashamed, or flat out embarrassed to the point we didn't want to risk negatively affecting the other with our words and memories. However, God gave us another shot at this marriage, and we opened up like never before.

Her Story

As we sat down together one Saturday morning, sipping coffee, I opened up to my husband with no distractions. I desperately want to have a healthy, intimate, sexual relationship with him. At times, it's there. We find the time to connect and experience all the bliss and intimacy sex can bring. However, other times, the feeling of shame stemming from the experience as a young teen creeps in. At those moments, I become closed off, and my husband senses my hesitation.

Until this conversation, he never understood what was going on with me in those moments. Since that teenage experience was an issue I quickly attempted to sweep under the rug of avoidance, my husband felt confused, rejected, and frustrated. However, during our open dialogue about sex, we talked about things we had never discussed before. We discussed intimacy, what we could do to stay connected, and discussed what the Bible says about sex.

Our Story

Scripture describes what a sexual relationship between husband and wife should look like in 1 Corinthians 7:3-5. Both the husband and the wife should yield to the other, not depriving each other unless mutually agreed upon for a time for devotion to fasting and prayer. Verse 5 specifically says that after a time apart for commitment to fasting and prayer, the husband and wife should come together again so that Satan will not tempt the couple.

Sex is the most intimate connection between husband and wife. It is key to maintaining a powerful bond. The absence of sex, for an extended time not mutually agreed upon, opens the couple up for trouble because the bond is not as strong. We experienced this in the so-called first half of our marriage. The weak connection between us left our marriage vulnerable to the enemy's schemes.

In a sense, not placing a priority on our relationship, including sex, left a window open in our home. The enemy saw this opening, crept in, and attacked. However, God had other plans. He restored our relationship, and we are now committed to safeguarding our bond. Allowing

God to be the center of our union and having open and honest dialogue serves as a security system to protect our marriage. We now desire to maintain the strongest bond possible. Therefore, it is our responsibility to ensure that we stay connected and maintain a satisfying sexual relationship, which we now view as a critical part of our marriage.

The honest dialogue that we had freed Yolanda from the emotional stress of bottling up the shame surrounding an ugly experience. The vulnerable and open discussion about sex connected us in a way we didn't even know possible.

Today, we both realize that we have needs - intimacy, connection, and sex. We now understand the real cause of the occasional roadblock to reaching our desired level of intimate connection. We are committed to working together to obliterate the roadblock. We are intentional about spending time together. We also openly discuss our desires and needs with one another.

In the past, we would drop hints about our wants and needs and get frustrated when the other person didn't pick up on those hints and act on them. As our parents used to tell us, "a closed mouth doesn't get fed." If we want something from our spouse and it isn't happening, we owe it to our partner to discuss the matter. We now put this into practice in every aspect of our marriage.

Couples often tell their spouse to "sex me more." We may receive advice from family, friends, and counselors to make sex a priority, schedule sex, and continue to date. However, sometimes it's a little deeper than only making time for sex. Sometimes some crucial conversations are needed. During these conversations, practical and honest communication comes in.

Our spouses must know our likes, dislikes, needs, and wants. They also need to understand our views on sex and our sexual history. Suppose we have scars, whether physical or emotional, from past experiences that may affect our sexual relationship. In that case, we owe it to our spouse to discuss these matters. As with most things in a healthy marriage, communication is vital.

As we continue to move forward in this new phase of our marriage, our goal is to fully understand one another. We are committed to making time for intimacy, keeping our connection as healthy as possible, and yes, to have more sex.

Today's challenge is to sit down and have an honest dialogue with your spouse about your sexual relationship. If you have a healthy relationship and are both satisfied in this area, let that be known as well.

Key Points for Discussing Sex

- Share your definition of intimacy with your spouse.
- Discuss your desires and needs with one another.
- Be honest and prepared to listen.
- Refer to scriptures regarding sex and discuss them.

Respond Here

Give specific examples of intimacy in your relationship.

_____

_____

_____

Read 1 Corinthians 7:3-5. What do you take away from this Scripture?

_____

_____

_____

Describe your sexual relationship with your spouse using five adjectives.

1. _____

2. _____

3. _____

4. _____

5. _____

Do you like what you see from the list of adjectives you created? Why or why not?

_____

_____

_____

_____

_____

Now that you have read this story, write a brief statement on how you can better address your sexual needs.

_____

_____

_____

_____

_____

_____

_____

_____

_____

_____

_____

_____

_____

Affirmation

I will challenge myself to sit down and have an honest dialogue with my spouse about our sexual relationship.

Scriptures for Further Study

Genesis 2:24

Therefore shall a man leave his father and his mother, and shall cleave unto his wife: and they shall be one flesh.

Ephesians 5:21

Submitting yourselves one to another in the fear of God. (Read versus 5:22-6:9)

Hebrews 13:4a

Marriage is honorable in all, and the bed undefiled:...

AFTERWORD

Each couple has learned much over the years. We don't get it right every time. Yet, how we engage, *connect* determines our outcomes.

The words spoken should have power and should build up each other. We should be able to share our needs, feelings, and dreams with our spouses. We must be mindful of the words we use. Having a heart relationship with God helps us to choose the right words that buildup.

Even if one must share something, the spouse did wrong. There is still a proper way to go about it in alignment with Biblical Scriptures.

This poem, written by a 15-year-old teenager, illustrates how children are always watching and learning.

What is Real Love

Love isn't always perfect;
it is no such thing as a fairytale
or a perfect storybook with a happy ending.

Love is fighting battles,
being together, and never letting go.

Love is a simple word,
but hard to define.

Those four letters can make
or break your whole life,
and you two chose to use them
to make your life.

So, let's not define love
as a word of affection,
but as a word portraying
your loyalty to stay together
through thick and thin.

The word love
defines more than how you look
at one another
when the sun rises over the horizon,
but as a word
to describe your bond
and life that you have built together,
for only love can exist
when two people put all things aside
to come together as one.

So, let us not focus
on the Perfect ending of love
because that is not the true beauty.
The real beauty comes from the accidents,
and the bumps in the road along the way,
for these mishaps,
create REAL LOVE.

Marriage Connection Prayer

(Insert your name in the spaces)

Lord, there are some days when I, _____ am not as gentle with my words as I should be. There are times when my thoughts spiral out of control. I, realize that Satan has a job to do and it is to try and destroy my marriage.

Help me, _____ to not create unnecessary friction between us. When I don't treat or speak to my spouse as best I know that I can. Convict me when I fall short. I, _____ will seek You daily.

Lord, I, _____ choose to love my spouse beyond myself. I, _____ will strengthen the bonds of both physical and spiritual intimacy in our marriage.

Lord, I, _____ will be kind and gentle. I, _____ will be forgiving and choose to stand strong through the shifts that may occur.

I, _____ will strive for peace in my home. I, _____ love You Lord. I, _____ will serve You and then my spouse and my family.

Amen

Anna's Poetry

William and Anna Roseboro

Making It Work Over Time

I Remember

I remember
Standing at the rear door of the
tabernacle That's the way it was back
then. If you're late, you have to wait.

I remember
Wondering where
   I would sit that night
I peeked around the usher
all crisply dressed in white.

The choir's still singing, and then
there's the opening prayer. The
usher won't seat me now, But, I can
check where.

Where will I sit? It's crowded tonight.
There are only two free seats in sight.

I remember
Thinking. Hmmm.
There's a handsome guy head over
there. A nice trim quo vadis none of

that hip Afro bush hair. I'm here for
worship, so, really, why should I care!
I remember
Weighing my options.
    Could I decide if or whether?
Where will I see him best?
    Where will he see me better?
I pat my hair and then straighten my sweater.

I remember
Choosing the seat in front,
not the seat right next to him.
How was I to know what would come
of that brief whim? It turned out
right, seated in his line of sight.

Well, fifty-six years later, we're still together.
Was it his neat hair or my snug sweater?

Well? Swell!

Once when the world was perfect
We decided we would marry
You were Nittany Lion and
I was a Warrior at Wayne
Marrying while we were in college
did not seem all that insane.

You were a basketball star.
And I was running track.
You were sending me
letters And I was writing
you back.

We didn't have cell phones back then,
So I never knew for sure just
when A knock on my dorm door
would summon me to the phone.
When we talked,
I felt like a queen on a throne.

All was going well, we both
thought the other was swell. But,
then you decided to break it off!

Then, all that what was heavenly
became more like hell.

Who was this woman who stole your heart?
Who was the woman tearing us apart?
Why would you leave? We'd made a good start.
Well, "Forget you," I said! But I couldn't, really.
Everything I recalled made me so touchy-
feely, That I whimpered at the drop of a hat,
Saying, "Well, that's that!

"It's over. It's done. We had a good run!"

Then you called me on my birthday!
I listened to what you had to say.
You said you were wrong to leave.
Would I, your apology receive?

Of course! I'd never stopped caring.
Though a heavy heart I was bearing.
I never gave up hope that we would marry.
But, believe me, I still will be wary.

But I was ready to drop the load and sing.
"By the way,
        when will you be bringing the ring?"

The Ballad of William and Anna*

Oh, it was around Christmas time
When the marriage, it was planned.
The family and friends all came to
see Lord William wed Lady Ann.

The musicians were seated,
all playing their songs
Awaiting the groom to appear.
And seated among the guests that day
Sat his former love, Lady Mear.

The minister signaled the groom to come
out To stand with best man at the right.
The minister motioned the guests to stand
As the bride marched in dressed in white.

Lady Mear, she stood with hankie in
hand Weeping for the man she had
lost. She'd been too proud to accept the
ring Lord William had gotten at cost.

The bride advanced at a stately pace By
her handsome groom to stand
Lady Mear, near the aisle,

Lady Mear, near the aisle,
Could be heard for a mile,
Shouting, "Hey, Lady Ann, that's my man!"
Lord William's response to the lady's
outburst,
"You had my heart in your hand.
You cast me aside. Yes, I did love you first,
But today, I'll wed Lady Ann."

So that day long ago about Christmas time,
The guests got more than was planned. An
old love turned mean in quite a wild scene
When Lord William wed Lady Ann.

—Anna J. Small Roseboro*
**Patterned after "Barbara Allen" Anonymous Poet
*Mrs. William G. Roseboro

Really?

Why did I really do that?
Was there another choice?
Did I consider the consequences?
Why did I listen to his voice?

Why did I take that chance?
Was I bored with life back
then? What if I had said, "No?"
Hmmm. Would I do this again?

What is it all about?
Why do I now want to shout?
Should I stay put or try to get out?
What is it all about?

Where can I go from here?
Will my friends still be there to
cheer? If I take a back seat
Will I still face the heat?

Was there ever another choice?
Should I have listened to his sister, Joyce?
Am I glad I heeded to his sweet voice?
Why did I really do that?

Our Son*

Baby, boy, grown
Robert, Bobby, Bob
Fast, fleet, flown

Born in a moment
Walking at nine months
Diving at two years
Gymnast at twelve

On the move
   On the run
      Seldom sitting
Often flitting
   Non-stop - ready to drop

Flying on his Big Wheels
Skidding under the bumper of
neighbor's Caddy
Cheating death, but
Barreling towards it

Building, building, building
Wooden kindergarten blocks
Golden Encyclopedia books
Cheerleaders' bodies
Blocks, Books, Bodies

Seeing the patterns
Finding the puzzle piece,
but
  Missing the picture
Moving on
  Moving out
    Moving up

High School
  Cheer Camps
  College

Sunnyvale Kinko's
Great Lakes Training
The Constellation in the Persian Gulf
The Juneau in Japan

Cheerleader
  Choreographer
    Cook – Chef

    Christian

On the move
  Flipping in time
    Hitting the groove
      Running out of time

Calling home
  Dad or Daddy

Mom or Mommy
The mood determines the name

Help or hooray
Sunny or gray
Seldom in between

"Do I have to come home?"
"Can I come home?"
"I can't come home."
"Now I have gone Home."

Baby, Boy, Grown
Fast, Fleet, Flown
Robert, Bobby, Bob.

*CS2(SW/AW) Robert Alan Roseboro,
USN
July 28, 1972- August 6, 2006

Anna J. Small Roseboro August 25, 2006

The Man with the Holes in His Socks

Sitting across from him on the sun porch
Noticing those holes in the bottom of his socks,

Listening to the birds chirping their evening
reports to their parents,
Hearing the squawk of the ducks as they

teach their ducklings to swim upstream,

I wonder what it would be like.

What would it be like to have no one to talk
to, no one to report to, no one to tease about
the holes in the bottoms of his socks; no
one to interrupt my reading with,

"Hon. You've gotta listen to this." Or
"Just a minute. Have you heard this one?"

Listening to the roiling of the steam just
outside the sunroom window,

Hearing the water tumble down the
man-made rock cropping,

Pausing as the mourning doves coo
across the way,

I wonder what it would be like.

What would it be like
to be able to finish a chapter

> without being interrupted,
> without learning something new about
> something I never knew was important,
> something I'd never even
> thought about before,

without realizing how fortunate I am
to hear from the man with the holes
in the bottom of his socks,

"Babe. This won't take long?" or
"Betcha never you hear this anymore."

Sitting across from him, I watch the
sunbeams streaming through the blinds,
slipping over his shoulder and warming
my toes, signaling that day is ending,
I wonder what it would be like.

Then, I smile to myself,
not having to wonder,
glad I don't have to wonder,
thrilled I don't have to wonder

What life would be like without the man
with the holes in the bottom of his socks.

Anna J. Small Roseboro, Summer, 2011

*Golden Anniversary Poem

We have been married now for fifty years.
True, some of the days have been cool and
blue, but more have been blazing gold.

Lying cradled in your arms, I feel
secure, cherished, and protected.

It's like being engulfed in Grammama's
handmade patchwork quilt.
Patches could symbolize states
in which we've lived,
the children we have
borne,

and the trips we've taken
from the Atlantic to the Pacific
in the car, on a plane,
or on that Amtrak train.

What adventures we've shared!
You know I tease you about your holey socks,
but it's wholly for fun.
I wish the same contentment in marriage
for our children.

Sometimes when I see the deer scamper
across the backyard,

I wonder if they enjoy their families
as much as we do ours.

Wandering wistfully,
    through the warm lovely home we share,

I gaze with a thankful, grateful heart at family
photos of siblings and their spouses, at dear
friends and grandparents who've gone on.

So, my dear, what lies ahead?

Whether smoky gray days or spicy peach days,
all will be better with you.
        Living by the Bible keeps us line.
I'm committed. We'll be just fine.

Loyal friend, husband for life,
It's been my joy to be your wife.

The Redwoods

Walking through Redwoods Forest
   with my Honey,
Standing among the majestic giants is worth
much more than money.

Who could imagine two hundred years ago,
When the seeds that first fell
   down to the ground
That two hundred feet
   up these trees would grow.
The awesome breadth;
   they're thirty feet around!

The crinkly quiet as we walk around,
listening for, but hearing no sound.
The twin trees leaning against each
other remind us that we need each
other To stand tall, so we won't fall.
Like the Redwoods, we must stand
fast to the last.

Oh God, we give You glory for it all.

September 2020

Pause and Ponder by Writing a Poem

---

*Poetry is "composed to convey a
vivid and imaginative sense of
experience, especially by the use of
condensed language chosen for its
sound and suggestive power as well
as for its meaning."*

Consider ways marriage partners connect and ways their faith support that connection, directly or indirectly. You've been reading the stories shared by the authors our editor has gathered for this anthology. You've scanned, maybe even read the poems I've shared.

Reread the opening quotation. This definition from the *Houghton-Mifflin College*

Dictionary is one I shared with my middle and high school students for decades. I invite you to pause and ponder your experience, observation, and or wishes for marriage and prepare to write a poem. Think of ways to convey a vivid and imaginative sense of experience.

You can do it. Sketch out a poem about one or more of the stories in this book, or a story of your own. Strive to convey your thoughts about a person, place, or event.

Or, try writing an acrostic poem. That's a poem in which a word written down the left side of the page is described by the words placed on a line to the right, beginning with each letter in that work. Draw or insert a two-column table. In the left column, write the letters in the name of the person, place, or event special to you or you connected with as you read. You may write about your partner, a place you visited together, or an event you shared. Next, choose words that begin with the letter on that line to describe that person, place, or event. Consider words that appeal to three to five of the five senses: hearing, smell, taste, touch, and sight. Consider words that sound like the ideas you want to convey.

Feel free to consult online alphabetical lists of adjectives, verbs, and nouns that will give you more ideas to consider. The kind of poem you will be writing is called an ACROSTIC because the specific letters in the left column make up the word about you are writing the poem. Just the first word in the second MUST begin with the letter in the first column. No other requirements. So have fun!

Here's a sample acrostic poem about connecting with my husband, William.

W	Wondering whether we will work
I	Ignoring irritation
L	Longing, loving, letting loose
L	Living, lounging, learning
I	Imaging incidental indicators
A	Analyzing, acknowledging, aiming
M	Managing to make it work

Finally, consider creating a greeting card for this poem using special fonts and images to help convey the message you wish to portray in ways that reflect the person, place, or event in ways that reflect the quotation that opens this section of this anthology.

Your Turn to Draft an Acrostic Poem

In the column on the left, write the letters of the first and/or last names of the person you would like to honor with your poem.

In the column on the right, fill in the spaces. The first word should begin with the letter in the left column. Including more adjectives, nouns, and verbs may be more fun!

Letter	Descriptive Words

Meet the Authors

John & Annette

David & Tanika

Terrance & Yolanda

Marriage
CONNECTION

...*making it work*
Faith-based Stories and Poetry

Compiled by
DR. ANNETTE M. WEST

Charles & Lekeisha

William & Anna

Mochamad & Mary

Tommy & Michelle

152

David and Tanika Blanding

Tanika D. Blanding is a native of Summerton, South Carolina. After graduating from the historical Scott's Branch High School, Tanika attended post-secondary college courses before joining the United States Army.

With more than 19 years of military service, she proudly serves as a Senior Non-Commissioned Officer in the rank of Sergeant First Class. Tanika holds several degrees in business and human resources. Currently pursuing her Master's in Human Resource Management, set to confer in October 2021.

Tanika is a Certified Instructor, Small Group Leader, and Master Resiliency Trainer certified by The University of Pennsylvania. Additionally, Tanika serves as a Licensed

Minister, Life Coach, Family Readiness Liaison, and Motivational Speaker.

David M. Blanding is a native of Brooklyn, NY. Growing up, David always had a passion for counseling and offering advice to those in need. This deep drive landed him in the career field as a Qualified Mental Health Professional for over 21 years.

David and Tanika were married on October 9, 2004. Together they have four children, two boys, and two girls. They are a power couple with a passion for helping others through sharing their testimony.

In 2016, David and Tanika founded a 501C3 (not-for-profit) Corporation called Creating Miracles, Life-Changing Corporation. The mission of Creating Miracles is to provide resources to underprivileged communities in an attempt to restore them to a better life. They also facilitate a podcast called "Till Death Do Us Part." This platform will allow space for vivid transparency and communication across the country. They will share individual and collective views on topics concerning the good, bad, and in-between ideas of marriage, ministry, dating, and other life areas that most have encountered.

Toni Henderson-Mayers
Author of the Foreword

Toni Henderson-Mayers is a relationship and business expert known as "Wise Courtship" because of her book with a 3-step system that helps you determine the true character and intention of your love interest. She has won the People's Choice, ACHI Magazine, Indie Author Legacy& Inspire Awards. Her work as Consulting Producer of the *Never Settle Show* with Mario Armstrong won an Emmy in the category of internet shows.

Take Toni's free course, "Finding Real Love" by going to bit.ly/findingreallove

Charles and Lekeisha Mosley

Charles Mosley is a native of Detroit, Michigan. During his over 30 years of experience as an electrical engineer, Charles continued his education by learning how to adapt to his new family and transition phase. Charles also discovered his passion for helping and teaching his young men how to be a thriving adult by being self-sufficient. Charles completed his education with a bachelor's degree at Oakland University and now works for the Department of Navy. Charles enjoys making crafts, singing, mentoring young engineers, troubleshooting electronic programming.

Lekeisha is a native of Detroit, Michigan. Lekeisha has earned a bachelor's degree in Business Management, and a master's in Management and Leadership. Lekeisha is an

Honorably Discharged veteran serving with the United States Army and Air Force. Besides being a full-time wife and mother, she works as a Radio/TV Personality of the Lekeisha Mosley Show. Lekeisha is a contributing author for the anthology, centered in Christ, and writes a daily devotion for the Facebook page, Lekeisha Mosley page, and podcast.

Charles and Lekeisha met in their hometown through close friends. They married and continue to raise their children in Maryland. After 8 years of marriage, the couple continues to adapt and grow from past relationships and have a new perspective of raising their family. While understanding how to create unique plans for a life together, Charles and Lekeisha are committed to not making comparisons within marriage and raising our three young men.

Products http://lekeishamosley.com/products/

Podcast https://www.spreaker.com/show/the-lekeisha-mosley-show

Facebook Page

https://www.facebook.com/lekeishamosley

Mochamad Usmanto and Mary Riley

Mochamad Usmanto is a native of Java, Indonesia. He came to the United States in 2015 to pursue his dream of opening a sushi restaurant. His dream was realized when he became Naruto Hibachi and Sushi's owner in Newport, Arkansas, this year.

Dr. Mary Riley is a native of Clarksdale, Mississippi. Mary has earned a Bachelor's degree in Human Resources Administration from Saint Leo University, a Master's in Education from Louisiana Tech University, and a Doctorate of Education from Grambling State University. Along with being a wife, mother, and grandmother, she works as the Director of Special Education within her local school district.

Mochamad and Mary met two years ago when Mochamad worked as a sushi chef at a local restaurant in Louisiana. After a brief dating period, they were married in 2019. Mochamad and Mary look forward to spending the rest of their lives together with God.

William and Anna Roseboro

Anna J. Small and William Gerald Roseboro met at their church camp in the summer of 1963. Second-year students at colleges in their home states of Michigan and Pennsylvania exchanged letters. They soon realized they would like to make a life together. However, they were committed to getting a college degree. Unable to afford to pay out of state tuition if either left home to marry and both remained in college, they agreed: Marriage had to wait.

Once married, they made their home in St. Louis, Missouri, began their professional careers, he as a chemical engineer, she as an educator, and began their family. Over the years, Bill and Anna have lived and worked in five states, borne and parented three children. They have faced the typical challenges of teenagers playing sports, taking music lessons, participating in church youth activities, and living abroad. Through it all, they have had good neighbors, loyal friends, and pastors who taught them to love and trust the Lord.

By the time Bill and Anna retired, the three children lived elsewhere. Their daughter settled in Chicago but traveled globally as a research analyst for international telecommunication companies and lived for a time in South Africa. Their oldest son joined the Air Force, served in Europe, remained there ten years, writing, performing, and recording as a rap musician. Back in the states, he became a music technology instructor in Ohio. The youngest son joined the Navy, served in the Persian Gulf, and rose to become Admiral's chef on a ship stationed in Asia. Then, they learned this son had died.

"How," folks ask, "have you managed to keep your marriage together with the myriad moves, multiple jobs, and now the mysterious death of your son?" First, Anna says, "We trust an ancient book, the Bible, as a practical guide to contemporary daily living. We respect each other and live in the paradox that the more space we give one another, the closer we become as a couple. Most important, we strive to maintain a personal relationship with God, our Creator; Jesus, our Savior; and the Holy Spirit, our Companion, Confidant, and Comforter. we generally live a life of wonder, not worry."

https://ajsmallroseboro.wordpress.com/

Tommy and Michelle Russell

Tommy and Michelle met in 1993 through a mutual friend and co-worker in Kingstree, South Carolina. They were joined in holy matrimony on July 3, 1995. In this union, God has blessed and entrusted them with five beautiful children.

Tommy is a native of Rochester, New York, and Michelle is a native of Kingstree, South Carolina. She was named at birth Michelle Brockington.

Both Tommy and Michelle Russell are ordained ministers. They currently serve at St. Michael Missionary Baptist Church located in New Zion, South Carolina, under the Leadership of Pastor Phillip Boyd.

They established a nonprofit organization called Pillar Outreach Ministry. Michelle is also a Certified Christian Life Coach who emphasizes a

Spirited led life and is approved by the HIScoach Training Academy Leadership.

God has commissioned Tommy and Michelle through prophetic utterance to "Enlarge the place of thy tent, and let them stretch forth the curtains of thine habitations: spare not, lengthen thy cords, and strengthen thy stakes;" (Isaiah 54:2). By doing so, the "Better Together Marriage" Broadcast will be established and launched in the year 2021. This virtual platform will allow both Tommy and Michelle to continue to use their God-given voice and influence to share God's wisdom and insight gained through their personal marriage experiences of "two becoming one flesh." Their sole purpose is to encourage, enlighten, and strengthen present and future marriage covenants through their union, relationship with God, and collaboration.

John and Annette West

John is a native of Jamaica, Queens, New York. He spent 22 years of active duty in the Air Force. John has a Masters in Information Systems Management and currently works as an Information Specialist (IT) for the government. He is a very reserved personality but watchful when it comes to me, who is often busy being the social butterfly. Thus, I may miss something going on.

Annette is a native of Hampton, Virginia, which is where she met John. She has earned degrees to her doctorate in Business Administration, with specialties in Management and International Business Relations. She is an ordained minister, college professor, pastoral counselor, holistic wellness life coach, author, publisher, and more.

John and Annette have been married for 36 years. They raised three babies, now all adults. Supporting the mission school in Kakamega, Africa, and prison outreach is essential to their purpose.

They live a quiet life, with a bit of chit-chat, walking, and bike riding together. In the evening before bed sitting close in proximity and saying nothing, a lovely atmosphere in the air.

https://drannettewestministries.org/contact

Terrance and Yolanda Whitehead

Terrance is a native of Hampton, Virginia. He is an Air Force Veteran and Retiree. During his 20 years of service, Terrance pursued his education, receiving a Bachelor's degree in Criminal Justice. Terrance also discovered his passion for serving his community through coaching youth sports. After retiring from the Air Force, Terrance went on to earn a Master's Degree in Public Administration. He now works with the military community as a contractor. He continues to work with the youth as a volunteer basketball coach.

Yolanda is a native of upstate New York. She has earned a Bachelor's degree in Business Administration and a Master's in Human Resources Development. Besides being a full-time wife and mother, she works as a Benefits

Specialist within her local school district. Yolanda is a contributing author for the anthology, Centered in Christ and writes a monthly devotion for the Facebook page, 30 Daughters.

Terrance and Yolanda are what are often referred to as "high school sweethearts." They married at the young age of 21 and now raise their two children in South Carolina. After 16 years of marriage, the couple separated and were headed towards divorce. During the separation, Terrance and Yolanda allowed the Lord to work on them individually. After some time, God restored their marriage. Together, their goal is to always keep it real when sharing their testimony with others. The couple now understands that marriage is work. Both are committed to learning and growing together to make their marriage the best it can be.

Other Books by Dr. Annette West

(2020) *Centered in Christ*, Editor

(2020) "Transformed Wholeness in God"
   Graced for It, Your Purpose Matters

(2019) *Holistic Wellness Mind Body Spirit*

(2019) *31 Day Journal Holistic Wellness Mind Body
   Spirit*

(2018) *Jesus the Path to Victorious Living*

(2018) *The Book of Isaiah: 23-Day Devotional*

(2016) *Living Words of Encouragement Vol 2*

(2008) *Basic Biblical Building Blocks*

(2007) *Entrepreneurship: The Godly Perspective*

(2006) *Living Words of Encouragement Vol 1*

Have questions, interested in writing your book, need coaching, or to be part of the next anthology contact Dr. Annette West at JATNEpublishing@mail.com

Sign up for our mailing list at www.drannettewestministries.org/contact.html

This book is: Spiritual -- Christian -- Daily Living –Devotional -- Bible Study -- Teaching Source -- Empowerment -- Coaching Resource

www.ingramcontent.com/pod-product-compliance
Lightning Source LLC
Chambersburg PA
CBHW070757100426
42742CB00012B/2173